My H
St. Michael the Archangel and the Dragon

A Devotional Journal

Season: _____

Date: _____

Belongs to: _____

My Holy Hour - St. Michael the Archangel and the Dragon is part of the *My Holy Hour Devotional Journal Series.* While all journals will have some similar structure and intent, each one will have minor changes to make it unique. Cover image depicts *St. Michael the Archangel and the Dragon*, Sienese, school of the 14th century found in the National Museum of Western Art, Tokyo, Japan.

Go to our website for a free copy of
How to Use a Prayer Journal during Holy Hour
www.HolyHourBooks.com

Holy Hour Books
P.O. Box 430577
Houston, TX 77243

My Holy Hour Devotional Journals

Cover Image by: By Daderot (Own work) [Public domain or CC0], via Wikimedia Commons

ISBN-13: 978-1-941303-48-1
ISBN-10: 1-941303-48-X

First Printing: 2017

Holy Hour Books is an imprint of Ordinary Matters Publishing.

Printed in the United States of America

Holy St. Michael, the Archangel, defend us in battle.
Be our defense against the wickedness and snares of the Devil.
May God rebuke him, we humbly pray; and do thou,
O Prince of the heavenly host, by the power of God, thrust into
hell Satan and all the evil spirits, who prowl about the world
seeking the ruin of souls. Amen.

Traditional Catholic Prayer to St. Michael the Archangel

My Holy Hour

Why Keep a Holy Hour

"First, the Holy Hour is not a devotion; it is a sharing in the work of redemption... our Lord asked: 'Could you not watch one hour with Me?'. In other words, he asked for an hour of reparation to combat the hour of evil; an hour of victimal union with the Cross to overcome the anti-love of sin.

Secondly, the only time Our Lord asked the Apostles for anything was the night he went into his agony... As often in the history of the Church since that time, evil was awake, but the disciples were asleep. That is why there came out of His anguished and lonely Heart the sigh: 'Could you not watch one hour with me?' Not for an hour of activity did He plead, but for an hour of companionship.

The third reason I keep up the Holy Hour is to grow more and more into his likeness. As Paul puts it: 'We are transfigured into his likeness, from splendor to splendor.' We become like that which we gaze upon. Looking into a sunset, the face takes on a golden glow. Looking at the Eucharistic Lord for an hour transforms the heart in a mysterious way as the face of Moses was transformed after his companionship with God on the mountain. Something happens to us similar to that which happened to the disciples at Emmaus. On Easter Sunday afternoon when the Lord met them, he asked why they were so gloomy. After spending some time in his presence, and hearing again the secret of spirituality - 'The Son of Man must suffer to enter into his Glory'" - their time with him ended and their "hearts were on fire." — Bishop Fulton Sheen

My Holy Hour

How to Keep a Holy Hour

"I have found that it takes some time to catch fire in prayer. This has been one of the advantages of the daily Hour. It is not so brief as to prevent the soul from collecting itself and shaking off the multitudinous distractions of the world. Sitting before the Presence is like a body exposing itself before the sun to absorb its rays. Silence in the Hour is a tete-a-tete with the Lord. In those moments, one does not so much pour out written prayers, but listening takes its place. We do not say: 'Listen, Lord, for Thy servant speaks,' but 'Speak, Lord, for Thy servant heareth.'"— Bishop Fulton Sheen

"Know also that you will probably gain more by praying fifteen minutes before the Blessed Sacrament than by all the other spiritual exercises of the day. True, Our Lord hears our prayers anywhere, for He has made the promise, 'Ask, and you shall receive,' but He has revealed to His servants that those who visit Him in the Blessed Sacrament will obtain a more abundant measure of grace." — St. Alphonsus Liguori

Holy Hour Pages

"The purpose of the Holy Hour is to encourage deep personal encounter with Christ."

— *Bishop Fulton Sheen*

HOLY HOUR QUOTES

"I have great reverence for St. Michael the Archangel; he had no example to follow in doing the will of God, and yet he fulfilled God's will faithfully."

— St. Faustina Kowalska

"And the time shall arise Michael, the great prince who has charge of your people. And there shall be a time of trouble, such as never has been since there was a nation till that time, but at that time your people shall be delivered, every one whose name shall be found written in the book."

— Daniel 12:1

"But I will tell you what is inscribed in the book of truth: there is none who contends by my side against these except Michael, your prince."

— Daniel 10:21

"Now war arose in heaven, Michael and his angels fighting against the dragon; and the dragon and his angels fought, but they was defeated and there was no longer any place for them in heaven. And the great dragon was thrown down, that ancient serpent, who is called the Devil and Satan, the deceiver of the whole world—he was thrown do to the earth, and his angels were thrown down with him."

— Revelation 12: 7-9

Record Your Favorite Quotes Here

REFLECTIONS

Personal Index

_____ *Pgs* ____

_____ *Pgs* ____

_____ *Pgs* ____

_____ *Pgs* ____

_____ *Pgs* ____

_____ *Pgs* ____

_____ *Pgs* ____

_____ *Pgs* ____

_____ *Pgs* ____

_____ *Pgs* ____

_____ *Pgs* ____

_____ *Pgs* ____

_____ *Pgs* ____

_____ *Pgs* ____

_____ *Pgs* ____

_____ *Pgs* ____

_____ *Pgs* ____

_____ *Pgs* ____

_____ *Pgs* ____

_____ *Pgs* ____

_____ *Pgs* ____

_____ *Pgs* ____

_____ *Pgs* ____

HOLY HOUR JOURNALS

Thank you for your interest in *Holy Hour Journals*. Discover more about using journals to deepen your prayer life by going to our website and getting a free copy of

How to Use a Prayer Journal during Holy Hour
www.HolyHourBooks.com

The Holy Hour Devotional Journal Series has been created to help Catholics from all walks of life to discover, explore, and enjoy the many rewards from a deeper connection to Christ.

Like our Facebook Page:
https://www.facebook.com/HolyHourBooks

Made in the USA
Columbia, SC
16 January 2024